The Lives of Rain

The Lives of Rain

by Nathalie Handal

foreword by Carolyn Forché

Interlink Books

An imprint of Interlink Publishing Group, Inc.
Northampton, Massachusetts

First published in 2005 by

INTERLINK BOOKS
An imprint of Interlink Publishing Group, Inc.
46 Crosby Street, Northampton, MA 01060
www.interlinkbooks.com

Library of Congress Cataloging-in-Publication Data

Printed and bound in Canada by Webcom Ltd.

*I am grateful to the editors of the following magazines and anthologies in whose pages some of these poems
first appeared:*
"Baladna," *Crab Orchard Review;* "The Warrior," *Ploughshares;* "Ephratha" and "Gaza City," *The Literary
Review;* "Presidente" and "Una Leyenda Invisible," *5 AM;* "The Uncertainty of Fear," "Twelve Deaths
at Noon," and "Orphans of Night," *Mizna;* "Kolo," *Stand Magazine;* "I Never Made it to Café Beirut,"
Folio; "Conversation with a Soldier" and "The Ballad of Haya," *Poetry New Zealand;* "Regrets in
Galilee," *Banipal;* "The Hanging Hours," *Perihelion;* "Pequeñas Palabras," "Une Seule Nuit à
Marrakech," "Tonight," and "War," *Blue Fifth Review;* "Strangers Inside Me" and "Dalmatian Coast,"
Respiro; "Jenin," *The Other Voices International Project;* "The Conflict," *Nthposition Magazine;* "The Lives
of Rain," *110 Stories: New York Writes After September 11* (New York: New York University Press);
"Bethlehem," *The Space Between Our Footsteps* (New York: Simon & Schuster); "The Blue Jacket," *A
Crack in the Wall* (London: Saqi Books); "El Almuerzo de Tía Habiba," "Detained" and "In Search of
Midnight," *Scheherazade's Legacy* (Connecticut: Praeger); "Around My Body, Lost Songs" and "Sense
and Sensibility," *Shattering the Stereotypes: Muslim Women Speak Out* (Northampton: Interlink Books);
"A Butterfly's Gaze" ("Milos Jovanovic's Dream"), *Post-Gibran* (Syracuse: Syracuse University Press);
"Even," *100 Poets Against War* (UK and Australia: Salt Publishing).

*

A warm thanks to the directors and composers who used versions of these poems in their work:
"War," was part of the dramatic work *Lost Recipes,* performed at Jump-Start Performance Co., San
Antonio (Feb 8–16, 2002); "The Hanging Hours" part of *This Song Cycle,* poems set to music by
well-known musician and composer Bruce Adolphe for Lincoln Center, The Rose Studio.

*

I would like to thank Elmaz Abi-Nader, Jenny Factor, Ram Devineni and Tina Chang for their
continued support and generosity. Deepest thanks to Ravi Shankar, Khaled Mattawa, Margo
Berdeshevsky and Myra Shapiro for their time and important suggestions. My heartfelt gratitude,
particularly to Naomi Shihab Nye, Ed Ochester, Veronica Golos and Carolyn Forché, for their
friendship and invaluable poetic insight. And to my sister Alexandra, endless thanks, for her artistic
advice and thoughtfulness.

Contents

III.

Foreword

In *The Lives of Rain,* Nathalie Handal has brought forth a work of
radical displacement and uncertainty, moving continent to
continent, giving voice to Palestinians of the diaspora in the
utterance of one fiercely awake and compassionate, who, against
warfare, occupation and brutality offers her native language,
olives, wind, *a herd of sheep or a burning mountain,* radio music, *a
butterfly's gaze.* It is a poetry of *never arriving,* of villages erased
from the maps, of *tattoed waistlines and kalishnikovs, a goat and a
corpse cut open side by side,* where *every house is a prison.* In a spare,
chiseled language without ornament, she writes an exilic lyric,
fusing Arabic, English, Spanish and French into a polyglot
testament of horror and survival. *Habibti, que tal?* she asks of
those who wander country to country, while those left behind in
Jenin, Gaza City, and Bethlehem inhabit *a continued past of blood/
of jailed cities.* Her subject is memory and forgetting, the
precariousness of identity and the fragility of human community;
it is the experience of suffering without knowledge of its end.
Handal is a poet of deftly considered paradoxes and reversals,
sensory evocations and mysteries left beautifully unresolved.
Hers is a language seared by history and marked by the impress
of extremity; so it is suffused with a rare species of wisdom.

—*Carolyn Forché*

For those who give us voice

There are some things about which nothing can be said
and before which we dare not keep silent.

—T.S. Eliot

The Doors of Exile

The shadows close a door
this is loneliness:
every time we enter a room we enter a new room
the hours of morning growing deep into our exile
prayers stuck in between two doors
waiting to leave to enter
waiting for memory to escape
the breath of cities.

I

Ephratha

There you stand
between the dream of two gazelles,
breathlessly
questioning the poem

Poem
dressed in olive branches and cracked happiness,
surrounded by seasons of sleepless nights staring
at the dusty walls of cities we have lost

Poem
that loses its address or that the address
loses, both, in either case awaiting
the return of those returning not today not ever

Poem
that wishes it could remember if the clouds split in half
the day the soldiers marched in our villages, towns,
houses, dreams and future, remember the crumbling of prayers
remember the gap between hands which held all
that the Poem was too weak to hold, remember when the horses'
secrets surrendered, when we trespassed ourselves

Poem
I ask you, why,
does the street have a name I can't pronounce?
Does our vocabulary invent us, our accents
resent us? Must we come to a halt
and try saying our name without feeling?
Try praising our poets without fearing?

Poem
is exile
a guest made of stones
a thin line between our voice and heaven's throat?

Poem
are our memories filled with pale notebooks,
fading paint, falling walls
to understand this place must we understand its howls,
to understand its howls must we understand its verses,
to understand its verses must we understand agony?

Poem
the murmur of rivers in your curved chest, the leaves
in your swaying arms, the sundering roof
the fields of wings, the dagger and the storm
everywhere inside of you

Poem
when will your words made of earth, your grotto of milk,
your wheat fields, monasteries, synagogues,
crosses and coffins stop stitching miles of bones, stop
broadcasting itself on the radio?

Poem
you stand between the dream of two questions
awaiting the day you will unfold yourself
like prayers unfold themselves from tongues,
you continue to stand, weep and celebrate
as if you were written
perfectly

The Conflict

They came as if I was not there—
thirty-three, one hundred and twenty-five
long hair, brown hair, blue eyes
lines on the sides of my mouth
yellow skin

They came while I was out buying bread,
not knowing that I walk
outside the house
without myself

It is not morning yet-
two ambulances, three fire trucks,
twenty-four cars passed in eighty-two seconds,
and they came

They came with death on their uniforms
perhaps we are not meant to understand everything,
so we try to understand
where we are from, where we are going,
what we look like

They came with a picture of a subway ticket
half a bottle of juice,
told me I can leave,
as if I need their permission
as if I am in the wrong place,
told me I wouldn't shiver when I sleep
or dream of moist earth
as if they knew me,
told me I didn't need to follow
misery at every corner
didn't need to see my sidewalks bleeding
as if that will change my mind

They came to tell me that
I do not understand the place I inherited
so they will help me leave,
and I realize—we are far from each other,
and grow farther still, smaller still
like broken glass shattered in our throats,
our breath abandoning God.

Bethlehem

Secrets live in the space between our footsteps.
The words of my grandfather echo in my dream,
as the years keep his beads and town.
I see Bethlehem, all in dust, empty
a torn piece of newspaper lost in its narrow streets.
Where is everyone? Graffiti and stones answer.
Where is the real Bethlehem—the one my grandfather came from?
Handkerchiefs dry the pain from my hands.
Olive trees and tears continue to remember.
I walk until I reach an old Arab man dressed in a white robe.
Aren't you the man I saw in my grandfather's stories?
He looks at me and leaves. I follow—ask him why he is going?
He continues. I stop, turn around, realize,
he has left me secrets between his footsteps.

The Blue Jacket

Stardust sifts on the shoulders of the blue jacket,
slides down to the end of the sleeves,
finds a place at the tower of my fingers.
I let the asterisks discover the heart of the sheet,
allow the ferries to travel wherever seaweed and lanterns
        call.
I think of the lovesong in the back pocket of a martyr,
the way he continued to walk until the end of the smoke,
remembered the white and yellow pack of cigarettes in his
        shirt pocket.
I knew that I could find color in the curves of branches
but all the color I wanted to see was in the blue jacket.
Subways and war games are afternoon attractions for those who
        survived,
I still live by the blue jacket's rules, its threads healed
        the bruises on the child's feet,
hid the only arak bottle left from the invaders...
The blue jacket. I wear it, so I will remember
the day I saw him in dewdrops, the day small ivory thorns found
refuge
        in envelopes
                of letters going...

The Warrior

It was Wednesday, I remember. Maybe it was Thursday. I had arrived early, early enough to drink some good wine alone with a man I thought we all should fear and for a second forgot. Then they arrived. Nothing in me had changed, even after the wine, even after I saw a goat and corpse cut open side by side. Some say this place is cursed, every drop of water sinks the earth. Strange the things one thinks about at moments like this—was I a stranger to the lover who saw my curves and scars, kissed them then slept like a deserter? Strange what comes to you in the dream-shadows of God—children you saw once in Nablus or Ramallah, who told you the hour the dates will grow in Palestine. Then they arrived. Announced—she died yesterday, but I heard she died a year ago, later that evening I found out she will die tomorrow. And then I heard him say, *Shut up, there is only one way to fight a war. Become the other.* I cross my legs and take his face apart trying to find a way to remember this moment otherwise.

The Combatant and I

It's been a long time—
where have you been, where are you?
I miss your frowns,
the dark shadow on your oval chin.
I can't breathe at night, can't feel my legs.
Dreamed I stopped seeing.
Are you lost?
Are you returning? Am I returning?
I suppose you would say,
I should be happy that I can still love.

It's been a long time.
Stop looking at me from so far, come to me,
stop following me, come to me,
through these dark alleys,
yellow-green forests, these hills of stone,
rows of olives and lives;
stop walking behind me, come to me,
you make me lose my way and ways…
I look out the window and think of
the shadows behind your shadows
we both don't recognize,
think that between us,
sleeps the words we had to leave,
think of the movement of hay twirling
on that breezy afternoon we crossed to,
somewhere
we did not expect to be.

Regrets in Galilee

A night by a fire, a day in Galilee
and all I found was a haunting
in the middle of your speech
a bridge of echoes…
I borrow the passion of birds for the evening
and trip over my dreams
like a woman wearing another woman's heels.
I think of the seasons that have offended me
and the lovers I never unmasked…
I let the running water flow on my lap
down my legs into my shoes.
What were you going to say
that night when I started traveling?
When I stopped you mid-sentence?

The Ballad of Haya

And a hand was left
nothing more of her
And the memory of
a bullet through
her uniform was left
nothing more of her
And the old gold color
of her hair
and the silver dark beneath her eyes
and the borders of her heart
falling as she walked
block after block was left
nothing else of her

Twelve Deaths at Noon

I look for their eyes, only see the dust
at the corner of their hearts. It's twelve o'clock. Midday.
Everything starts here. The sun heating our foreheads.
The arrival of a murdered son or husband. The bullet
they vow to find. The voices like drumbeats in our ears.
The strangeness of light between these boys and their stones.
The prisons in our souls. The rivers dying in our mirrors.
When was the last time we looked at our reflection
and saw ourselves, not jars of eroded bones
not the small child in us looking for our burnt eyelashes.
When was the last time we slept without dreaming we died,
without wishing the killer dead, without looking for our gun
while making love.

I pass tanks, soldiers, orange blossoms,
look at the earth, wait for a message a song.
Hear nothing. The land lies bleeding. It's noon. The boys,
now angels in stone, have come back to a different home.

Jenin

A night without a blanket, a blanket
belonging to someone else, someone
else living in our home.
All I want is the quiet of blame
to leave, all I want is the words from dying tongues
to fall, all I want is a row of olive trees,
a field of tulips, to forget
the maze of intestines, the dried corners
of a soldier's mouth, all I want is for
the small black eyed child to stop
wondering when the fever will stop
the noise will stop, all I want is
a loaf of bread, water
help for the stranger's torn arm,
all I want is what we have inherited
from the doves, a perfect line of white:

                              where are the bodies?

Conversation with a Soldier when no one is Around

When no one is around
I change my address.
Can't change my face
give my father freedom
my brother peace
so I change my address.
Change trains
to keep me going
bring me back.
Change lovers
to keep me coming
keep me going...

When no one is around
I see the book about
to land on the wet floor
but do not pick it up;
can't leave myself alone.
There are secrets we
can't leave unguarded,
secrets we don't
even know we have...

When no one is around
and a child is shot dead,
what will the fighter
or the soldier do, what did you do?
Who cares but the mother
and the father, who are dead
who died yesterday, a while ago,
who knows, no one was around...
were you around?

When no one is around
who will answer your questions—
take your time, don't answer right away,
no one is around to hear you,
I am no longer here
no one is around
you know that.

When no one is around
the leaves
dye the earth the color of Fall,
a fall we never see coming.

Gaza City

My hands and my check against
the cold wall, I hide like a slut, ashamed.
I pull the collar of my light blue robe so hard
it tears, one side hanging as everyone's lives hang here.
My fingers sink deep into my flesh,
I scratch myself, three lines scar my breasts,
three faiths pound in my head and I wonder
if God is buried in the rubble. Every house is a prison,
every room a dog cage. *Debke* is no longer part of life,
only funerals are. Gaza is pregnant
with people and no one helps with the labor.
There are no streets, no hospitals, no schools,
no airport, no air to breathe.
And here I am in a room behind a window,
choking on my spit.

The Uncertainty of Fear

We weave tiny heavens between our prayers,
between the lips of dying soldiers, *a warning*
the roads are not lit, the way obscure,
but we continue anyway, looking for
the tide in our voices
the words death forbids us to repeat,
the musicians who play the 'oud or the lute
the pregnant women without shoes
the objects we kept from Room 242-
a remote control, a red ashtray, a pillowcase, toothpaste-
nothing we need. We continue without asking
why this small silence, this bitter wind,
this cold darkness blocking our lungs.
Then we stop, and *try to tell each other something.*

Detained

For Mourad and all those unjustly detained
in Palestine and elsewhere, and to Ghassan

Over a cup of Arabic coffee
back in nineteen ninety nine,
on a balcony in Ramallah,
we spoke of the *situation*,
how we survive, *we don't*, you said.

We had more coffee
your hand trembled
your trembling revealing
the years you never saw go by
the wait jailing you
your wife and child...

Three years later

you are detained...
I imagine a cell as tall as you—
five foot eleven inches,
as wide as you—
twenty-one and a half inches,
life reduced to your body
your memory of light,
the whisper of your wife sliding
under the slim opening
of the iron door, to remind you
that you must not forget these hours
who you were, are—
we forget too easily
keep changing back to ourselves...

But brother, don't be jealous
of another's memories,
don't be jealous of your memories,
just remember what they
have done to themselves—
that the darkness they have planted
in our bones will cripple their bones,
that detainment is their life sentence,
that their blood staining our graves
is a stubborn witness.

Haifa, Haifa

We were from the East
and then we escaped
left the coast
broken walls
dusty roads
nightmares
the place we were born and
where we died.
Now we keep hoping we might hear
what we want to hear,
live the way we should live...
The lemon trees keep disappearing
and the weather keeps changing,
we keep aging
keep coming back
but never on time
to see those who keep leaving.

The Hanging Hours

When I leave, the windows will be shut
the air in the room will turn moist, the city loud,
the telephone will not stop ringing, the electricity
will go on and off, the coffee will be brewing
and everything will continue

When I leave the sky will dress in light blue
before wearing black, the people I know
will have tears flowing from their eyes to their hands
before they wipe them off and continue

The bed I leave will be warm
the other body will not know I am missing
until the very next day when the hours hang
and he finds himself,
in a mild season, in a wild place
where breaths crowd the bedroom.

I Never Made it to Café Beirut; Nor, I Heard, Did You

You told me that I should wait
at the Lebanese border. You told me not
to fear the Hezbollah, the gunshots,
the missiles or grenades, told me

that I would not see the shadows of corpses
in the stained grey clouds, would not see
the refugees and the UN trucks waiting for God.
You told me that no one would

be singing war songs, or speak of
liberation, Saddam, Bush, the Israelis.
You said nothing about the trumpet of flames,
the shattering glass.

You insisted, meet me at the Lebanese border.
Told me to bring my favorite poems
of Baudelaire and Gibran, my dreams
wrapped in my black hair, my questions—

the ones you could not answer at the time,
the simple facts—your real name, age, nationality—
and also why the night was held in siege,
why the souks were so quiet, the mountains

so quiet and the dead still struggling.
And why I had to meet you at the border.

II

Une Suele Nuit à Marrakech

The air has lost the scent of jasmine.
Darkened tea fills the sky.
Tonight in Marrakech, only white butterflies
leave stains on shadows.
I watch a young woman brush her hair,
braid her wedding day, watch old men gather
by the lemon trees, listening to Andalusian tunes
repeating, *Hel'lou, qu'elle belle musique.*
Handsome gentlemen drink coffee
from small cups, an aroma mapping
their homeland, stones and ceramics
dark blue, light blue, turquoise…
It's springtime but I return to my hotel room,
turn on my lantern, eat honey pastry, *kab el ghzal*,
drink mint tea, later *arak*,
watch lights dim against my bare feet,
start to count and lose count
of the wild shape of darkness,
the marionettes and war games,
tiles hiding the shadows
of those I no longer want to see,
and the *abayas* piling by my bed side.

Orphans of Night

We stood under the doorframe,
you on one side, me on the other...
we were used to borders.
It was Paris seven o'clock.
Café des États-Unis.
I felt the night under my blouse
and waited for you to greet me.
My map around my neck
you ask me if we come
from the same place-
where figs lie on the coffins
of boys, a past misplaced.
You give me a glass of red wine
ask me who killed my father
tell me why the nights
begin every night here
and lead me to a stroll.
We walk through avenues
unknown in our stories
reach the Metro
turn to each other
wanting to return
returning only to an empty
bottle of wine and a café
about to close.

El Almuerzo de Tía Habiba

Half past six in the morning
the kitchen is wide awake,
no time for many cups of coffees
for Tía Liliana, Tía Mercedes,
Tía Rosette, Tía Esperanza,
Tía Josefina, Tía Margarita,
Tía Layla and Tío Wadie
are coming for some of Tía Habiba's
tamalitos, lamb, hummos, laban, and grape leaves.
"Dios mío niña, you are not dressed," Juanita tells me.
Her Indian features recite poems her ancestors tell her
the way Tía Habiba's deep curved eyes
tell me about the holy land.
"Por favor, it is not morning yet," I respond.
These are what my Friday mornings
are like when I visit my relatives in Torreón, Coahuila,
a little ciudad in México.

By noontime, everyone has arrived,
voices crowd every room.
Before I go downstairs, I stand
at the top of the staircase looking
at those people below as if I were
on the Mount of Olives looking
at the Old City, and I wonder
how these people got here,
so far from the Mediterranean sea,
the desert heat. Now they are caught
between Abdel Halim Hafez and Luís Miguel,
jelabas and sombreros, lost in the smoke
coming from the *arguileh.*
I start going down the stairs, hear
them say, *Habibti, que tal?*
and know that all has changed.

Caribe in Nueva York

Un Caribeño tells me:
we are spoiled here
we eat burgers, fries
arroz y habichuelas negras, plátanos
for two dollars and ninety-nine cents
others starve, looking for a few bits—
We forget hunger...
I love America
but I dream of mangoes
Café Santo Domingo, merengue,
salsa, bachata, son
I can't forget the sun on my back
in my eyes
but this is Nueva York in winter
and I can't see the beautiful brown legs
of *las mulatas*
can't see their curves as they move
in the streets of Brooklyn, Bronx,
in the Upper West
Washington Heights...
Now I eat at Lenny's Bagels and Gray's Papaya
I look at the Hudson
instead of the Caribbean waters, *los malecones.*
Proud of Gloria, Shakira, Mark, JLo
Juan Luís Guerra, Celia Cruz...
I dream of *la tierra*
where we were born,
I walk Central Park
with our islands in my pockets
and my gloves on.

Baladna

We are who we are,
and home is home
to keep the seasons dreaming
to remind us of
ahweh, zaatar, khoubiz, kaak—
the common things

I am no longer sure what I see:
a field of wheat or a field of olive trees,
a herd of sheep or a burning mountain,
not sure if it matters
now that I stand alone
at the corner of a small road
somewhere between my grandfather
and what seems to be my present...
Am I as old, as young,
as sad, as torn, as strange, as sorry
as those I have lost?
I try to remember all that has been offered to me:
winkled bed sheets, library passes, old passports,
ports we stopped at for an hour...
we are who we are; are we who we are?

We write a ballad to celebrate ourselves, *baladna*
and wonder, is that what it's like
to dance in Arabic...

Blue Hours

In the blue hour,
the *negrita* cries, I hide
not to deceive the darkness
or myself...

La negrita is not far
from where I stand
her eyebrows
her one hand...
I too am visible now, behind the tree
behind the night, behind the cry
and all I want to know
is her name
and ask her:
have you ever heard
your heart undressing,
seen a stray dog at midnight,
realize he understands this hour
better than we will understand any hour?
have you seen yourself in every woman
with your eyes or in women with eyes
more difficult than yours?
have you ever really heard your voice,
echoing in your nipples?

She offers me tea,
we end up drinking coffee,
trying to reach the bottom of the cup
unafraid....

now, my teeth are stained, my English
failing me, my Arabic fading
my Spanish starting to make sense…
we are in a *finca* now—
perhaps we are safe,
perhaps we desire nothing else,
but I can't stop bowing in prayer
five times a day,
my country comes to me, tells me:
Compatriota—I will always find you
no matter what language you are speaking.

Strangers Inside Me

We all have reasons
for moving
I move
to keep things whole.
               —Mark Strand, "Keeping Things Whole"

Outside, the quivers of winter,
a sudden moistness, a slow darkness.
Outside, strangers looking for themselves
in the silent motion of my handwriting.
I stand at the corners of night
hoping that violets will remain purple in winter.

There is a country on my tongue
a small world between my heartbeats.
Strangers inside me that understand
the strangeness of strange things,
that understand they are not strangers
to each other but it seems strange to
others that they belong together, as if
we can refuse ourselves ourselves.

Words slide down my throat
like velvet rivers and outside
a tiny echo is calling me
as I travel and move
from one continent to the next,
move, to be whole.

In Search of Midnight

He kissed my lips at midnight
        I let him
He took my blouse off
        I let him
Took my bra off
and touched my breast
        I let him
He took my pants off
        I let him
Took my underwear off
and looked at me standing
in this strange, dark
black and white room
        …I let him
A small light dimmed
by the window
I took a glimpse of
the city we live in,
both do not know…

Then he pronounces
my name wrong
        and I stop him…
Ask him if he has ever
been exiled or imprisoned
if he has ever mailed
letters to a woman he
once loved but would
never see again
if he thinks we can go back
to a lover even if
we might not love
the second time,

asked him if he ever
robbed a small grocery store
or stole a bread from a peasant,
if he has ever crossed
seas, coasts and mountains
and still could
not arrive...

He answers:
I did not pronounce my name
correctly in my country
so I was tortured,
I did not pronounce my name
correctly at the enemy line
so I was exiled
I did not pronounce my name
correctly upon arrival
so I was given new papers...
You see. A heart in search of midnight
is only a heart, everything else is the same,
except what the other is expecting...

Dalmatian Coast

we speak of weddings
you speak of funerals
we understand each other

who has survived
don't answer

we tell each other
don't lean backward
don't bend forward

Around My Body, Lost Songs

Before soldiers and dictators
invaded the bridges over the Euphrates,
before speeches haunted our dreams
and army trucks scrolled their wheels
deep in the heart of Iraq,
every evening was evening in Baghdad.
elegant, convincing, orange skies seducing
neighbors reciting Al-Mutanabbi,
women smoking *sheesha*, dancing a small dance,
coping with the terror buried in the dark lines
under their eyes.

Before tonight, the lost songs
danced around my body.
But tonight the desert blows at the desert looking for itself
the storm enters the storm to chase the invaders,
bombs explode the sleep of children
leave them orphaned, hungry, leave
them collecting skulls, bodies of victory...

Tonight the sky's colonized
where will heaven go?
The earth a battlefield
the new refugees refusing their new destinies,
running away from their shadows,
running toward Babel, toward the Arabic language
well preserved
un-cracked
until now, until then,
lover—don't you understand?
I did not die even if they killed me,
I have forgotten everything
just so that I could never forget

Kolo

In the Balkans
a woman breastfeeds, hums a low tune, combs her hair,
laments hanging on the village trees, she tries to forget
the rapes the refugee camps the slit throats
of Srebenica, tries to remember the blink of her own past passing,
days dancing the *kolo*, each torture unsung in that violet swaying.

Unsung, the slow movement of a foreign language
on the lips of an émigré, the sailing of cruel memory in water drops
drying on the cover of a book with Cyrillic letters.
Unsung, the swallowing of sentences by soldiers
after they have killed...
She imagines those who have left, the search for lost relics,
silverware in ordinary antique stores in Paris London Chicago
looking for anything an exile leaves
except the song unsung beneath the tongue of the sea wind...a *kolo*.

A woman breastfeeds and cooks and hums,
crosses fall sideways without a sound,
the past slips beneath her raised arms,
the *kolo* whirling on.

Goran's Whispers

travel through evenings of choking riverbanks,
dying lime trees, through memories
of soldiers who look past each other,
and have forgotten their own faces,
through memories of death and broken hourglasses.
Goran whispers, *why must we witness*
the fate of small things as they vanish in screaming
grounds, witness their speech before their end...
They cry out, *klaonica* and they repeat *klaonica*
repeat *klaonica* repeat and repeat *klaonica,*
as if it was the only word they could remember, their only testament,
then their words like their bodies become ashes
in a graveyard behind the broken streets, broken houses,
broken hospitals, behind the empty stores, empty fields,
empty voices, behind the terrified children and their
terrifying games terrified of the terror inside of them
and the entire world seems to have lost Goran's whispers
somewhere in their memory of yesterday, now all seem
to exist in bruised skies. In conversations people have of the past.
Except for those without a house. Without clothes. Without silence.
Except for those souls still screaming beneath the ground.
Afraid that they will be killed over, and over again.

The Lives of Rain

The old Chinese man
in the health food shop
at 98th and Broadway tells me
the rain has many lives.
I wonder if he tells everyone
the same thing or if this is something
between us, wonder if he fought any wars,
killed anyone, wonder if he ever fell in love,
lost a house, lost his accent, lost a wife or
a child in the rain, wonder if he calls for
the rain when he stirs his daily soup,
wonder what hides in his silk cloth—
rice, pictures, maybe memories of rain.
Rain he tells me, carries rumors of the dead,
of those with suitcases and epidemics.
Rain carries the memory of droughts,
of houses gone, rain like lovers
comes and goes, like soldiers go
and sometimes return to a life
no longer standing.
The Chinese man waits for me to ask—
who really knows how many lives to come.

War

A cup of empty messages in a room of light,
light that blinds; blinded men lined up
the young are unable to die peacefully, I hear a man say.

All is gone: the messy hair of boys, their smile,
the pictures of ancestors, the stories of spirits,
the misty hour before sunrise
when the fig trees await the small hands of a child.

Now the candles have melted
and the bells of the church
no longer ring in Bethlehem.

A continued past of blood,
of jailed cities
confiscated lives,
goodbyes.

How can we bear the images that flood our eyes
and bleed our veins: a dead man, perhaps thirty,
with a tight fist, holding some sugar for morning coffee.

Coffee cups full
left on the table
in a radio station
beside three corpses.

Corpses follow gunmen in their sleep, remind them
that today they have killed a tiny child,
a woman trying to say, *Stop, please...*

a single man holding on to his prayer rug,
holding on to whatever
is left of memory...

listen, how many should die before we start counting,
listen, who is listening, there is no one here, there is nothing left,
there is nothing left after war, only other wars.

Pequeñas Palabras

It all ended here
between Abraham Lincoln and John F. Kennedy
our disagreement about wealthy liars and poor thieves
left at the corner of these two avenues, left
the way we leave an unfinished sentence hanging
if we think it might betray us, left
the way we leave the awakening of morning
in a place we do not recognize, left
the way we leave our country rising
from a dream—its *ríos, colinas, llanuras*
the way we leave the radio
our grandfather and father listened to
leave the barbershop we passed in front
everyday empty usually empty
left the way we leave it all one day
except the haze of a rainy afternoon
and the words we know best:
cerveza, comida, música, miseria, amor.

Sense and Sensibility, Contemporary American Politics

We sensed that you made sense,
but sometimes, we have to sense
these things out,
and wait for everyone else to
come to their senses...
I have since realized that
no one is going to come
to their senses
and
nothing makes sense...
But please,
correct me if I make no sense,
if it makes sense
that we now publicly
can announce that
in the name of sense
we are being sensible,
in the name of sensibility
they must all die
for the world to make sense
and for us to regain
the consensus that,
it is not senseless to kill
it makes sense
in order for our world
to regain order and sense...
Come on—can't you see,
we need sense in our lives
to continue living this non-sense.

Presidente

I pass avenues, boulevards, streets:
Abraham Lincoln, George Washington,
John F. Kennedy, Winston Churchill,
Charles de Gaulle and stop at a *colmadito*
and ask for a "Presidente."
"Eso si, en este país Presidente es la mejor."
I am tempted to respond but instead
take the very cold bottle of beer and leave.

Suddenly, all I see are barrios and beggars,
graffitis and broken streetlights, children barefoot;
all I hear are the dead walking in-between trees-
flamboyanes, amapolas; and pausing in front of
orquídeas, anturios, flores de caoba,
and I wonder if flowers are what they miss most,
if they are the shadows on my tongue,
wonder as the last crossing of scents pass through—
sugar-cane and cinnamon, alcohol and tobacco
guava, mangoes and oranges—
if all Presidentes create such confusion.

The ocean's breeze lightly slaps my tired face
and I see a man with a cold steel bucket
coming towards me selling *Presidentes*.
I ask for a new one.

Even

Nothing is even, even this line
I am writing, even this line I am waiting in,
waiting for permission to enter
the country, the house, the room.
Nothing is even, even now
that laws have been drawn and peace
is discussed on high tables,
and even if all was said to be even
I would not believe for even I know
that nothing is even—not the trees,
the flowers, not the mountains or the shadows...
our nature is not even so why even try to get even
instead let us find an even better place
and call it even.

Una Leyenda Invisible

A legend floats in the light blue river
while the roots of trees scream
la noche desaparecerá
and strangers walk shoulder to shoulder with ghosts
not realizing how crowded the world is,
how hungry, how dry the river

A legend floats in the deep blue river
a woman with seamless lime eyes
never looks at the daylight reflection
in the water, never questions why
the river is sometimes light sometimes dark

A legend floats in the indigo blue river
a hatless man leaves his ear piece
his maps his books his memories
his exile his half-forgotten name
on a bench by the river, but never looks at the mist

A legend floats in this river in Lima or Barranquilla
in Quito or Caracas, but no one really knows
how the legend goes or how it floats
except most say, there is no river
no legend.
They never look.

Milos Jovanovic's Dream

The night floats, the world chokes,
a sip of betrayal stuck in my throat...

I walk in Milos Jovanovic's dream
barefoot
with jokes under my feet, tears in my skirt pockets...

I walk in a shallow midnight battle, toward a falling treetop
a drizzle and its cane, a memory
a memory caught in jasmine and standing whispers...

I walk in days of strangeness murmuring
beside columns of space murmuring—
echoes and ghosts belong to the same world...

A world surrendering
surrendering
for the nights are floating

and we continue   remembering...

Tonight

water will reach
the rim of the glass but will not
allow itself to leave the glass

violence will erupt and horrors
will tie themselves to
every bare tree

tonight we will hear speeches
that tell us to open our legs
to scandal like whores

tonight we will see
tattooed waistlines and kalashnikovs
in the back trunks of cars

paralyzed memories and
revolutions behind
every house door

we will see red landscapes,
stones of light, light feathers swaying
in the nightscape

and wrinkles will multiply
on our faces tonight as each
dead rises from its grave

tonight exiles, immigrants, refugees
will be caught in songbirds,
cracked asphalt will recite old verses

tonight we will listen to the cracks of narratives
the screams of those strangled
by the night at night

we will listen to the longing
of purple evenings
under god's robe

tonight love will be difficult.

III

Amrika

I

The Curfews of History

Distance keep us in its wake;
our half deserted streets
keep impossible equations,
Fedayeens and Mujahaddins,
the Old City, Sittis and Jiddos,
nights all night digging,
digging for body parts,
for anything that was once part of them—
arm, leg, finger, a sliver of hair

Without water or prayer, we continue
walking to all the borders we can reach
somewhere—different each time.
We are neither breath nor death,
we are a body of holes,
a skull of silence

witness the gaze
the bruised child, the throat
of our national song,
our heart stopping time
as we leave our conversations
in a broken ashtray
somewhere in this divided country

women weave, weave
thread after thread,
lost songs of Palestine, Oum Kulthoum
buildings built and torn down,

the way home changing as the city does—
with every bomb, a new wall.

The years grow taller
past the unopened doors,
we continue to dance, hands swaying
the air, *Ya Allah, Ya Allah,*
we will never leave.

II

The Tyranny of Distance

From Jaffa to Marseille:

How does one begin to understand the difference
between *Sabaah el khayr* and *bonjour,*
the difference between the city of lights and black-outs.

C'est comme cela, tout change habibti,
but our names stay the same,
our eyes remain, our memory.

I sing *Inshallah* in French as I walk les banlieue Parisienne,
walk through Barbes, Bercy, St. Denis, Rue Bad-el-Oued
uncertain, looking for what I am most certain of.

Wait for my lover in Nazareth
whom I write to years later:

Love, you never saw my hair grow out
or did you see me cut it?
You never asked me about the men
I betrayed for you, nor did I ask you
about the window sill that held the hissing

58

between our lips, a glass of wine shattered
on the cement floor
silence broken in a room
too small to survive.
We were lost again,
this time we did not pretend,
we were prepared for our tendencies.

Will we ever smell the sweet scent of morning
in Haifa again,
remember the faces who never slept in our bed.
Is your throat swollen with history?
They divided us.
Dead Sea. Trenches. A verdict. A verse. A voyage.

Never mind. Tell me the color of your hat,
if we will arrive on time for death.
Je n'ai jamais oublie
ce que tu n'as pas cesse de me dire,
la terre ne ment jamais.

III

The Cry of Flesh

Et Maintenant, les Antilles.
The ticking of tombs,
abandoned
somewhere we never find,
between
the dance of darkness
in the island of Boukman, tap-taps,
Tabou Combo and Sweet Mickey,
in the streets of Port-au-Prince-

Ayiti cherie, plus bel pays—
Cité Soleil, where the sun forgets
and people compete for the heavens,
with baskets on their heads
perfectly balanced
walking at all speeds
counting their steps their days,
hoping to find God
in the poor hands of another.

I leave with the Kreyol—
tioul, zonbi, refijye, testaman, ma lé—
leave the soft drumming of shadows
leave our sleep: we did what we had to,
but it was not enough.

IV

Opening

New England
quiet echoes raindrops autumn leaves
an alley of tiny butterflies
the difference between where we are from
and where we now live.

The years behind a broken door
my father's grief—
I understand nothing—
only later do I hear the Arabic
in his footsteps...

I walk through Fenway Park, through
streets with names that escape me,
their stories of sea

their cries for a stranger's grief.
I understand—no one can bear partings.

Only the stationary I left in that apartment
remembers what I might
forget to say, but time looks different now,
it wears another hat and owns a car,
and we are comfortable in foreign tongues
but the music that continues to move us
is a melody from the east—
an opening of whispers in our shivers.

V

El Color del Inmigrante

We land somewhere we recognize—
the Spanish language, rows of *inmigrantes*
playing dominos, drinking rum,
paint peeling
secrets falling on floors,
we reach the Miami beat,
Cubano dreams and South Beach,
la revolución, Azúcar,
carnivals, hurricanes and superstitions,
speak about *la tierra de Dios*
while living in a tower on Collins,
where everyone visiting
is considered suspicious
a word we know
a reality we understand—
leaving, we survive.

VI

Another Sun

Too many highways,
we head south
Santo Domingo—*isla dulce,*
listen to Bachata, Juan Luís Guerra,
speak about Sosa, El Camino Real,
las calles en la Zona Colonial

where priests and witches
small hells and bitter plains
live between the hours
between the cracks of doors
between conjugations of verbs
we do not know in the past
or future tense
but keep practicing...

and behind *edificios* and *torres*
are *barrios*, a world of *blakao, apagón*
stillness splitting, portraits of a daily war,
the stains of ashes, of dust between lips.

We leave mosquitos and mamajuana,
pack our pictures
the sweet taste of sugar cane,
the caress of coconut in our mouth,
as if we can hold on to everything we pass through,
as if we can remember our past,
think of our future as if it is sure to come.
Why do we insist
on disappointing ourselves—
past or future

suspense or dream
instead of hoping the present.

VII

Incantations

English verses and riverbanks at midnight,
uncover the broken vases of whispers
hidden in Shakespeare's country

as I cross the different faces of the wind,
a past I passed in words and dreams,
Yeats and Beckett, smoking *sheesha*
on Egdeware Road

the mist, a room I could disappear in,
the odd colors found in Portobello Market
a way into – a small muse in London

where I came to know
the silent rain inside of me
as the Thames had come
to the rhythm of my breathing.

VIII

Debke in New York

I arrive. In New York
witness barbers
cutting the hair of men
faces vanishing without
returning for morning coffee

shadows on my forehead
war in old newspapers
frost on the winter windows
the past a bedroom I once slept in.

I wear my jeans, tennis shoes,
walk Broadway, pass Columbia,
read Said and Twain,
wonder why we are obsessed
with difference,
our need to change the other?
I wait for the noise to stop
but it never does
so I go to the tip of the Hudson River
recite a verse by Ibn Arabi
and between subway rides,
to that place I now call home,
listen to Abdel Halim and Nina Simone

hunt for the small things
I have lost inside of myself—
and at the corner of Bleeker and Mercer
through a window with faded Arabic letters
see a New York *debke*...

It is later than it was while ago
and I haven't moved a bit,
my voice still breaking into tiny pieces
when I introduce myself to someone new
and imagine I have found my way home.

Notes

(In order poems appear)

"Ephratha": Ephratha is Palestine's Canaanite name, meaning "the fruitful."

"Gaza City": *Debke,* traditional Arabic dance.

"Une Suele Nuit à Marrakech": *hel'lou* means beautiful in Arabic; *qu'elle belle musique* means what a beautiful song in French; *kab el ghzal* is a honey and nuts pastry, otherwise known baklava; *Arak,* an alcoholic drink; Marrakech is situated in the center of the Haouz plain; *Abayas,* long robes, typical in Morocco.

"El Almuerzo de Tía Habiba": *almuerzo* means lunch in Spanish; *arguileh* is a water-filtered smoking pipe.

"Caribe in Nueva York": *arroz,* rice; *habichuelas negras,* black beans; *plátanos,* plantains; *son,* typical music from Cuba; *los malecones,* waterfront boulevards; Gloria, Shakira, Mark, JLo, Juan Luís Guerra, Celia Cruz are all Latino performers/musicians; *tierra,* land.

"Baladna": *baladna,* my country; *ahweh,* coffee; *zaatar,* a mixture of toasted sesame seeds, dried thyme, sumac, and salt; *houbiz,* bread; *kaak,* Arabic cookie.

"Blue Hours": *negrita,* little black woman; *finca,* farm; *compatriota,* country woman, compatriot.

"Around my Body, Lost Songs": *sheesha,* water-filtered smoking pipe, also known as arguileh.

"Kolo": kolo is a round dance, an important aspect of Balkan folklore.

"Goran's Whispers": *klaonica* in Serbo-Croatian means slaughterhouse, butchery.

"Pequeñas Palabras": *pequeña,* small; *palabras,* words; Abraham Lincoln and Kennedy, two main avenues in Santo Domingo, Dominican Republic; *ríos,* rivers; *colinas,* hills; *llanuras,* fields; *cerveza,* beer; *comida,* food; *música,* music; *miseria,* misery, poverty; *amor,* love.

"Presidente": *colmadito*, small convenience store; *Eso si, en este pais Presidente es la mejor*, "That's right, in this country Presidente is the best; *flamboyans, amapolas* are kinds of trees; *orchedeas, anthuriams*, and *flor de caobas* are flowers.

"Una Leyenda Invisible": *La noche desaparecerá*, The night will disappear.

"Amrika": *fedayeen*, one who sacrifices his life for a cause—martyrs; *mujahaddin*, freedom fighter—he fights in the name of god-*jihad*; *sittis*, grandmothers; *jiddos*, grandfathers; Oum Kulthoum, one of the most well-known female Arab singers; *Ya Allah*, Oh God; *c'est comme cela, tout change habibti*, that's how it is, all changes sweetheart; *Inshallah*, God willing; *Je n'ai jamais oublie, ce que tu n'as cesse de me dire, la terre ne ment jamais*, I did not forget what you never stopped telling me, the land never lies; Boukman, a statue in Haiti which symbolizes the revolt of the slaves in 1971; *Ayiti cherie, plus bel pays*, Haiti darling, the most beautiful county; Cité Soleil, a poor area in Haiti; *Kreyol*, Creole; *tioul*, slaves; *zonbi*, ghosts; *refijye*, refugee; *testaman*, testament; *ma lé*, I'm going; *inmigrantes*, immigrants; *revolución*, revolution; *azúcar*, sugar, and the well-known Cuban singer Celia Cruz always says it when she sings; *la tierra de Dios*, the land of God; *isla douce*, sweet island; *bachata*, type of popular music in Dominican Republic; Juan Luís Guerra, well-known Dominican singer, composer; *edificios*, buildings; *torres*, towers; *barrio*, slums, ghetto, quarter, suburb; *blakao*, slang for blackout; *apagón*, blackout; *mamaquana*, alcoholic beverage made with rum and herbal roots; *debke*, typical Arabic folkloric dance.

About the Author

Nathalie Handal is a poet, playwright, and writer, who has lived in Europe, the United States, the Caribbean, Latin America, and the Middle East. She finished her MFA at Bennington College and her post-graduate degree at the University of London. Her work has appeared in numerous magazines, literary journals, and anthologies worldwide, and she has been featured on NPR, KPFK, and PBS Radio. She has directed and is the author of numerous plays; and of *Traveling Rooms* (poetry CD), and *The Neverfield*. She is the editor of *The Poetry of Arab Women: A Contemporary Anthology*, an Academy of American Poets bestseller and winner of the PEN Oakland/Josephine Miles Award. Handal is presently working on two theatrical projects, finishing a short story book, editing two anthologies, *Dominican Literature* and *Arab-American and Arab Diaspora Literature* (forthcoming, Fall 2005); and co-editing along with Tina Chang and Ravi Shankar *An Anthology of Asian and Middle Eastern Poets*. She is the poetry review editor for *Sable* (UK) and associate artist and development executive for the production company, the Kazbah Project. She teaches at Columbia University.

Also by Nathalie Handal

The Neverfield

An emerging young talent in the field of poetry and culture, Nathalie Handal writes with great passion and eloquence on the subjects of displacement, diaspora, and the search for cross-cultural identity.

"The Neverfield is a work which insists on itself. It is poetry of a shining quality from a poet whose voice is sure and unafraid."

—*Lucille Clifton*

70 pages • ISBN 1-56656-595-2 • pb $12.000

The Poetry of Arab Women
A Contemporary Anthology
edited by Nathalie Handal

"These are poems both of revolution and evolution, emerging from the ancient, rich but exclusionary tradition of poetry in Arabic. Thus they enlarge the domain of poetry itself...May this book receive the attention and appreciation it truly deserves."

—*Adrienne Rich*

"...a world long silenced discloses itself in a symphony of lyric utterance at once passionate and profound... Beautifully researched, translated, and compiled, this book is necessary to any appreciation of world literature in our time."

—*Carolyn Forché*

384 pages • ISBN 1-56656-374-7 • pb $22.00

To request our complete 40-page full-color catalog, please call us toll free at **1-800-238-LINK**, visit our website at **www.interlinkbooks.com**, or write to
Interlink Publishing
46 Crosby Street, Northampton, MA 01060
e-mail: info@interlinkbooks.com